Copyright

All rights reserved. For now. For the first 10 years of publication, please don't steal this book and try to make money off it. Buy *lots* of copies for friends and for your local library. See the URL at the bottom of this page for the latest permissions.

This book is entirely a work of fiction. The names, characters and incidents portrayed in it are the work of the author's imagination. Any resemblance to actual persons, living or dead, events or localities is entirely coincidental.

Please review this book and thank you for supporting independent authors. And do me a favor: take good care of yourself today.

~Matthew.

Poetry Works, Mostly

*poems good enough
for the likes of you*

by matthew oliphant

Introduction

I got a bee in my bonnet over the last weekend of October. One could argue, adroitly, that I was avoiding doing other things, but I think putting together 90% of this book over 2 days counts as being productive.

I went through old hard drives, notebooks, and the web to find all the poetry I've written. It's not a lot, about 60 or so, but it was fun looking for them and revisiting some I'd not thought about for a few decades.

This book is sort of a "collected works" edition. Some of the poems I've worked hard on and some of them were written in less than a minute. I think I tend to like those the best. There are one or two that I set out to do something very specific and I think I accomplished that.

Could they all be better? Of course. Getting through the final 10% took another month.

Are any of them great? One is.

I could work for another 30 years on some of these—that's how poetry goes. But at some point, to steal a phrase from dayjob-land, you gotta ship it.

This book is a word temple.
At least, it wants to be.

I hope you like the book you are about to read, even if it isn't this one.

Content

A thought I thought

When you think a thought
The more you think a thought
The more that thought you think
Even if the thought you think is thoughtless
Or not well thought through
Or cruelly untrue
To others or to you

Think of thoughts you think
Be thoughtful,
but not overly so,
lest thoughtfulness leads to thinking
thoughts
you think you would not like to know

A boat that's far away

There's nothing quite like a boat that's
far away
Meandering down a river or
sails unfurled at the mouth of a bay

Walking the rocky shoreline
minding the sail's silhouette
more than where I place my steps
I want to go where it is going
Rising and falling from swell to swell

But if I was there
I would not be here along the shore
My feet rising and falling from rock to rock
I would not see the boat that's far away
and be able to appreciate it
to marvel at the view
imagining journeys and destinations
which I will never know

The Seven Seconds of Oboe

Sitting before the red, raging fire,
that fire,
with new-found and long-time friends.

Talking and laughing and longing,
that longing,
at times with intentions best left unsaid.

And then she handed me an oboe.
And I played, (much to their chagrin)
and played,
and played.
Until I found those seven seconds.

Those seven seconds,
those seven seconds,
those seven seconds.

The fire stopped.
The talking and laughing and longing,
even that longing,
all stopped for seven seconds.

Three Cents Short

There is a roll of not-forever stamps
in the glove compartment.
Not many on the roll, perhaps ten or so.
They've been there for years and
they are stuck together.
Years of heat and
years of cold
have bound them into a ring.
A never-ending line of three-cents-short,
sticky pieces of paper and
they are worthless
for any sort of correspondence delivery.

And it reminds me of us.

Random Poetry Generator #3

Wine absorbs a shower of our
sex-blind fall.
Spring, in sheets of coffee
Winter, private jolly,
blessed, onerous apple.

Saved in you—
A Summer and
Autumn of laughter.
Your mistress is your Saint.
Onerous living,
onerous journey.
I blink and miss our kiss

Song note: love is yours.
Melon mornings only.

Around 1995, I made a Random Poetry Generator using TinyMUSH code. Yeah... I'm old. The format was fixed—six words in the first line, three in the second, and so on—but each word had a 1-in-N possibility, where N was the number of words I entered. There was no API for a dictionary back then. I entered a few hundred words and would run it over and over to see what I got. The third one was pretty okay.

I added the punctuation and capitalization, but other than that it was random—within constraints, naturally. Like, apparently, the code really liked the word: onerous.

Mon Oncle

Mon Oncle, Mon Oncle non
I remember him fondly by the fire,
resting out the evening in his rocker,
entranced by the crackling embers.
I meditated on thin smoke and mulled wine,
and felt the moments of that day, fleeting,
as my mind fell toward the moments
of so many tomorrows.
A resonant snort signaled his rousing.
The spectacles,
perched on his knee,
fell to the floor.
He hesitated a moment,
then gave them up for lost.
I would have reached for them.
A soft, slight chuckle.
I saw he was smiling at me,
his eyes half-open,
left eye wandering.

I can still hear him as I rest in his rocker,
entranced by the crackling embers,
spectacles just out of reach.

Pallbearer

Leveling off at the required pace.
Inclined at the proper angle.
Descending to the appropriate depth.
Enclosed in this moment,
unprepared.

Green and black squares mark
the way.
Haggardly walking,
sweating of nerves.

Brown slate beneath
the green-black flowers
and squares of
brown and tan.

Hypatia,
hippogryph,
hardly moving.

Memories and Junk

I am cleaning my desk.
Stacks have sat stagnant here
for a long time.
Things that were important.
Things that needed to be taken care of have
become lost opportunities.
I waited too long.

I am throwing away memories.
It is one thing I am very good at.
I throw away three letters from an old friend
who used to be very important to me.
The most important at the time.
I throw her away.

Piles of memories.
Pictures of me with a blue face,
with a tired face,
standing next to a happy face.
A face I once made happy for a few weeks.

Pictures are the vestiges of my
thrown away memories—I have many of
them.
Not enough to visually document my entire
life,
but enough for a general overview;
enough to jog the body into
an emotional reaction.
Less so over time.

When I throw away the pictures,
I throw away the last of the memories.
I might be reminded of them once in a while.
Like when my parents told,
"When Matthew was a kid..." stories,
I can vaguely imagine a static image
of what they are talking about,
but it's not the same as remembering.
I am remembering
their story
and not the event itself.
It's not a real memory.

My house is cluttered with objects
that represent memories.
A bunch of junk for the most part.
And yet I lug it with me from place to place.
I used to be able to fit all
my memories into a backpack.

Now I am married.
My parents are no longer around.
My wife with her memories, I with mine.
Vestigial piles of maybe memories from my
parents.

We live in a house filled with memories.

So quickly becomes junk.

Some of it is still valuable,
but all of it will, someday,
end up like
the letters,
or the picture

of a blue-faced me,
or the bulk of my parents' possessions
in a black,
plastic trash bag
with convenient
yellow handles.

Water

I am a young boy now.
My skin is dark and smooth.
I wear the clothes of my people.
We spend our days in and near the desert.

I have been a young man.
In Egypt or Sudan, I face north.
Is there water to the east or the west?
How far?
I might choose the wrong direction.

Once I was a man of worth.
Camels and rugs tell of my success.
I have not moved in some time.
Others bring water to me.

Long ago I became an old man.
I am a burden to my people.
My camels are dead.
My rugs are tattered.
My skin is dark, but wrinkled.

This is the time of the choosing.
Tell me the path to the water.

I had a teacher, long, long ago, whose first name was so long, it didn't fit on his drivers license.

He said, "People call me Fox." He was from Egypt. Or Sudan. Likely near the border because the stories would change from time to time.

He taught me how to levitate, and I wrote this because of and for him.

Objectively, Truth is Subjective

I hold no truth to be self-evident.
I only assume.
Perhaps I surmise, though to be honest, I am
not sure what the practical difference is.

"All men are created equal."

I recite the words I have been taught.
I think the dependent thoughts I have been
told to think.
I cannot think of anything I know to be true.

We would, as a society
—or even just the two of us—
get nowhere if there weren't some
assumptions.
But I assume everything.
I never have the impulse to seek truth.
No, not true.
I have the impulse,
but not the motivation to see it through.

No interest beyond
smashing shiny thoughts together
like particles in a super-collider.
Ooooo... Got a rubber pencil going.
Maybe it's ADHD.
But if you have ADHD, do you really have the
attention span to stop and wonder if you have
an attention span problem?
You do?
I see.
What was I saying?
reads up
Ah, yes.

No truth is self-evident.
You have to go looking.
You have to work for it.
You have to be curious, mostly, but
judgmental enough to know when you have
found it and when you have not.
Assuming truth exists.
Surmising.

"All men are created equal."

The criteria by which one can be considered
to have been created equal
is apophatic.
Which is apoplexing.
Even then, that which is included
within the borders of the pleasant
salamander
still seeks to define a sense of otherness,
cloaked and hooded
—or not hooded, if you were born after
1968—
in...
checks notes
Epistemology.
I'm sorry, I meant
competitive penis measuring tournaments.

That can't be right.
checks notes
Huh. Weird.

For the record, sometimes a
rubber pencil
is a
rubber pencil.
What was I saying?
reads up
Ah, yes.

In an "all men are created equal" world,
in the long run,
it's probably best to stay on this side
of the velvet rope.

But it is also probably best
to hop across once in a while,
when no one is looking,
to grab a bottle of
whatever champagne is *en vogue*.

His Sighs

He sighed with the weight of his troubles.
Sitting on the edge of the bed,
His feet halfway in his slippers.
The morning ritual.
Sigh,
slippers,
sigh.

Stagger to the bathroom.
Shower, shave, lean forward to see the weight
on the scale.
"It just won't come off."
It will be years until he is diagnosed
with a thyroid problem.
Pop some pills and the weight rolls right off.
Until then, his sighs are his only escape.

Her Commitment

The woman screamed, "Asshole!"
The cab drove away quickly,
leaving her in a heap on the side of the road
with a broken arm and a mangled bicycle.

She managed to
curse and drag herself
to the emergency room two miles away.
She was wet, dirty, and bleeding.
And she was in so much pain.

They fixed her up clean and good.
She thanked them and
apologized for all the profanity.
They understood.
Pain is like that.

Her bike was totaled.
They offered to call her a cab for the ride
home.
She didn't pause,
walking straight out the door.
"No fucking way."

Rose 1

My love is a rose of
many colors.
Each Saturday night
I wander the town
to dive bars
and Mexican restaurants.

I knock on the windows of taxis downtown,
and wait outside
movie theaters for
starry-eyed men and women.

I carry my basket
into birthdays
and anniversaries;
to one night stands
in the lobbies of
cheap motels.

I move with the energy
of the evening,

selling my love
to new faces and
old alike.

They take my love;
I take their money.
It is a healthy exchange.

I carry my basket of colored roses.
I carry my basket of love.

Rose 2

Velvety rose petals
fall from my hands
conveniently close
to the spots
I most want to play

She Loves Me, She Loves Me Not

I pluck the first petal
from her shoulder.
Tracing it up her neck
to her cheek, placing
it gently
on her outstretched tongue.

She loves me.

Another from her breast.
Covering her
deliciously wrinkled
nipple, collapsing

around and pulling up,
lifting both into my mouth.

She loves me not.

From her forehead,
brushing across
each eye,
down her nose, into her
waiting mouth.

She loves me.

From her soft knee.
Then up her leg,
back and forth,
moistened
with the wetness
between her thighs.

She loves me not.
From the sheets, but resting

lazily against her side.
Across her quivering
middle, up around
each breast a full circle, spiraling
up her throat,
across her smiling lips.

She loves me.

From her left hand,
grasping and releasing
the sheets.
Up and down each arm,
so slowly,
not quite a tickle.

She loves me not.

I take the last petal from her hair,
spread out across the pillow.
Down the center of her, adding
more pressure as I go.

Delving, swishing
back and forth, leaving
the petal just inside.

I reach in with my tongue,
darting in and out,
to pull the petal
into my mouth.

She loves me.

Rose 3

The brittle petals fall to the floor
with my hesitant caress;
I ask forgiveness.

I try to save this wilted form,
to put back what has been lost.

Do not trouble yourself, you say,
that rose has been dead for many years.

Is Down Out?

I am drowning again.
That quagmire pulsating with heat
and such a familiar cadence.
Submerged unwilling,
(or willing?)
down to murky depths.
Blades of long dead grass entangle my body,
stopping the circling of blood.
Mire forces itself inside me.
Filling every pore, every orifice.
Lungs ravaged until they almost explode.

I see nothing, feel nothing, breathe no air.
Yet, I do not die.
"No, never that,"
speak voices from below
echoed from above.

I see it all in my mind.
Away now, watching and crying,
not able to control my body

as it threshes about grotesquely
unable for anything but fear.

"No escape, save to wait for the end."

I have been trapped here so long,
I do not think I could breathe real air,
or look upon anything brighter than
this dim cocoon I have made.
(Or was it made for me?)
This place which both crushes and
spreads out endlessly; là-bas.
This place where there is no next.

But for that singular voice.
Cleaning my ears,
wiping my mouth,
purging the muck from within.
That voice!

Calling down to me,
"You can breathe this air.

You always could."

I open my eyes and gasp and
cry to see a hand, so lovingly
held down toward me,
lifting my chin and shielding
my eyes from the sudden light.

My legs *schpluck* as I am pulled
from that dim place—
a place in which I had become
far too comfortable.

An open, smiling face
that has always been
accepting
and wanting to help.

Einfach or Another (I'll Get You)

I don't want
to be the receptacle of
your blind, zipper love.

I Saw My Dentist

I saw my dentist at the gas station today.
I said hello and he politely greeted me in
return.

But he didn't recognize me.

Which is not all that strange
considering my soul is rotten, too.

A Different Path

It rained on Sutter Street
as we walked along,
hand in hand,
beneath the budding trees,
past an old white horse whose elevator
door doesn't close correctly.

Then up the hill a bit to that double rainbow
and fill our stomachs with life.

Laughing
and
running
my heart is filled with joy,
by you,
as we race through this field of dahlia,
spreading
our arms wide to excite the flowers;
falling
pollen in our wake
coming

to rest on newfound love.

Later, the afternoon sun warms us.

The leaves have mostly fallen
to the ground, but a few find purchase still.
The sky is cast over gray,
sheet-like and still.
There is the scent of recent rain.
I sit, calmly
watching
people pass outside my window,
thinking
of you.

Red lines of time shine on my face.

Staring
in silence, I remember
days past, now
passing.
I sit amongst three clocks

(which are less than more in sync)
in a room adorned with memory.
But, there is something here I cherish above all,
an item for which I would give up my
dependency on time.

Simply, a pressed dahlia.

I list and listen
to the steady syncopated
ticking.
I feel, again, the
pounding
of my heart.
The arrival of your hand,
offered across the void,
striking
through the wall between.
The warmth of your last touch felt through
my shirt spreading
to the reaches of my self,

recognizing
the tender gesture, complimented by your
smile.

To feel this closeness and this touch.

I lay alone in this room.
Both doors are open now.
Brash sounds drift down the hall
entering
this place; they are offensive to my solace.
But I am drawn to a particular sound.
A final whisper—your name.

I smile at the surprising simplicity of this final
moment.

For MEH.

Cascabel

Sometimes used fresh, more often
the Mexican cascabel is dried
into a reddish-brown sphere
the size of a walnut
with paper thin walls and jingling seeds.
It has a smoky, tannic bite.

*Found poem. I noticed in a clipping from the
local paper on my fridge titled, "Sorting Out the
Peppers" whose quoted source was "Hot Licks" by
Jennifer Trainer Thompson, Chronicle Books.*

Love is the worst

I can no longer engender
gut-wrenching hurt.
Not sorrow,
nor pitiness,
nor perturbation.

I've lost touch with things
that used to be
so important to me.

I couldn't care less
now what grieves me.

For I know love and happiness
(feelings admittedly new).

It is hard to remember
how to instill
lament in my poetry.

Love is the worst.

tekau ma rua hekona e moemoea ana

Sitting and leaning
back in my roller chair,
a shiver runs up my spine.
From tail to top and back to the beginning.

Again I have taken a tumble—the red light
doesn't blink.

It is me and not me.

Again I can see it coming. Likable.
Like the pattern was set ahead of time;
flatware in position.
Register.

Splicing together little sighs and dead spots.
Tangled web.
It is true: *Ich meine. Tata.*
I had better take out the garbage.
Money, lots of money. And for what?
My mistake.

Wrong cab.
Can't this side, won't that.

Waiting and waiting—the red light still
doesn't blink.
Can't run.
Head shake.
Big sigh.
No more.

Lisboa

Leaning out this chilly sill,
my face is washed with light
from above,
and my imagination
teased with melody
from below.

Time to Leave

As we left together,
I thought this trip
might prove troublesome.
Across the creek and up the hill.
Rising and falling
along winding paths to see
cascading copper,
water-carved rocks.
Then up and up and up
we climbed
to sit atop a grassy knoll and
speak wismaticies,
which you assured me is a word.
Talking and listening
while the sun fell
each wondering
what the other must think.
Then came the question,
near the end,
on which we made a statement
as we left apart.

A Life Between Breaths

Between us have been
exchanged just simple greetings.
As shall ever be.
And yet, I have felt
your soft lips brush my shoulder
caressing more love.

Haikumiko

Wind blows through the grass.
Our blanket under the tree
food still left untouched.

For Yumiko

Hm

Casting aside an antiquated belief system.
Establishing a belief system.
Adapting a belief system.
Adopting a belief system.
Antiquating a belief system.
Making others believe in your antiquated
belief system.

The three of us are part of a larger group.
Ben and KP more than me.
We occupy three of the four chairs at the
table.
The fourth chair is for those who wander by
and have a few moments to stay.
Ben is looking for a job.
KP is putting up fliers about an AIDS
awareness rave.
I am avoiding my inertia.
"Someday we'll be the ones in charge," I tell
them.
Ben doesn't believe me.

We belong to an elite group of semi-
professional by-hook-or-by-crooks.
We shuck responsibility, try to live
paycheck to paycheck
even without a job.
We are all wanderers.
Wanderers with direction, mind you,
but the direction can change at any moment,
for any reason,
And someday,
we'll be the ones in charge,
because no one else will want to do it.

Each Time I Travel

An impossible Tundra,
frozen and parched for life.
On the rise, is it perhaps the
Wind through the lifeless
Tree that calls me here?
But
not
quite
lifeless, perhaps.
Each visit brings renewed hope of a welcome
Spring.
A few blades of green grass at the base; a
budding leaf on a branch.

An estranged tone
sends shivers through me
and again I feel the chill.
The moment when the tone ends
and the silence begins,
I wonder if Spring will come.

Sweaty Psalms — Jesus #1

He said I looked like Jesus.

I took him at his word,
but didn't initially have
a worthwhile response.
He stared up at me.
I looked blankly down at him.

Finally,
I said,
It runs in the family. I look a lot like my dad,
but I get nervous speaking in public.

Jesus Just — Jesus #2

Jesus just walked into the bar.
He's wearing a jacket that looks like the one I
lost last year. The guy on the stool next to me
agrees; it looks like a jacket he lost once, too.
Same thing with the bartender. We describe
the thing differently, but it's definitely the
one.

Jesus just ordered a drink.
He asked the bartender to make it a double.
He's drinking the same as the rest of us. It
tastes different, but it's the same.

Jesus just buried his face in his hands.
He's got the same problems as me, the
bartender, and the guy on the stool next to
me. We know this 'cause he just laid out his
problems to the bartender and we all looked
surprised.

Jesus just went over to the dartboard.
He made a bullseye, but only after missing
the entire board three times. None of us plays
darts.

Jesus just made a pass at the server, Margie.
I've done that. So has the bartender, many
times. The guy on the stool next to me was
going to do it when the timing was right.

Jesus just walked out of the bar with Margie
in tow.
Man, what a louse.

Water in Her Wine — Jesus #3

She was at a social gathering when a man caused a scene.

She found the water in her cup had turned to wine.
She didn't really like wine and felt the man should have asked first.

She feels that the taste of wine is too strong, so she went next door, where they still had water, and added it to her cup.

She likes water in her wine.

She has lived through many ages since. The Fall of Rome. "It sounds like it was really bad, but there were some pretty good years." Wars. Conquests. Plagues. She lived through it all.

She likes water in her wine.

The Middle Ages. "Talk about dark...whoever thought light could be such a commodity?" The Age of Reason. "Those Greeks really knew how to live. Unfortunately, what they had to teach us didn't translate very well." The Industrial Revolution. "Whoever thought light could be such a commodity?" The Gilded Age. The Space Age. The Information Age.

She likes water in her wine.

She likes to water down most everything. Most would say it takes the flavor out of life. She says it makes it all last so much longer.

For Marisa—that she should live forever or at least until she is done.

Was This a Moment?

This is a moment
as is this
and this
and this

Sitting on this beach
I watch the waves work away
I feel the rocks and sand beneath
me and
they are comforting

Resting on these rocks which keep
me held to this spot as
I am nowhere else

Walking from the surf is an Asaro Mudman
he points the tip of
his spear in
my face and says in a language which
I cannot understand

Searching far and wide for
my long-lost soul has brought
me here. Might
you be
he

Crying
he is sullened as
I reply

I am not
I have been lost only a short while

The Spiritual Awareness of the Political Nature of Everyday Life; Including: War, Ants, Butterflies, and Possibly Trees

I've never understood ants in their
working ways
or butterflies
as they flutter by.
Trees I can almost understand.
I've felt trapped before, too.
Haven't I?

"Indeed. Pray, what manor beast
beset thee, now bested?"
I stand now triumphant,
like an elephant,
in this forest—
long yet lost of those never forgotten
not forgetful
in contest, uncontested,
yet beaten.
Don't I?

"You seem discontent
with the content
of this life."
I understand nothing I stand over,
syncopated in my sycophancy.
Alone, I am mistaken in which
I have taken well enough.
Fewer ants work.
Fewer butterflies flutter by.
I look again and not a tree in sight.
Where am I?

"You are and have been here."
And this is where?

"It is a dream."
I stand still,
steadfast sure
the rain will come again.
Will it?

"It will not."

Poli-babel

As any neo-geo-political secular humanistic analyst of post-revolution symbolism and/or expressionism would tell you, in reference to the antithetical nature of the arts, humanities, and intercultural relations of right-wing government conservatism: the proposed stock pre-committal decision to postpone current revolvatory discussions about future of full scale public and private funding of collective monies to be distributed on the basis of need, not to be out done by the unrefined political push from the left to raise certain grants or endowments for budding young artists who have demonstrated a seemingly invaluable flair for determining the zenith of their own cultural movement into mainstream constructionism, propels congressional leaders from all points west to re-examine their stance on the horizonical nature of the so-called rigors of a political spin dry that has, until the Voodoo Economics of the Reagan era, taken its toll on many a long winded, and quite uneventful, term of office.

Snake and Poodle

Last night, as I watched the full moon through my fathers binoculars, I saw a snake offer a poodle a nice, delicious apple beneath a palm tree.

It seemed to me as though the snake were being quite generous. First for giving the poodle shelter from the old-day light. Then for giving him a nice, delicious apple to eat.

Or perhaps the poodle was just too smart to be fooled into giving the snake what he wanted, "I shan't eat this nice, delicious apple, snake. Why not give it to the people down there?"

The people had been there only a little while, but the snake thought that it was not such a bad idea, suspecting the poodle would have no use for a car.

The people never said much on previous visits, but the snake found that after eating the nice, delicious apple, they had very much to say about how bad the traffic always seems to be and that conventional wisdom dictates to always avoid the 5.

The snake went back to the poodle—still shading himself from the old-day light with the fronds of the palm tree—to show him the core of that once nice, delicious apple.

"This is very curious," said the poodle, "they might never be quiet again."

The snake agreed and said, "I was right to suspect that you would have no use for a car."

Take That, Joyce — Artifact 1

I have taken the razor
From a cross
his mirror
Long
Sharp
Straight

What was once this man's
—*Introibo ad altare Dei.*
is now an artifact for the pallet

I am
making the rounds
of relief

Take that, Pound — Artifact 2

Record of a struggle,
"... of himself, as a man with struggle."
Periplum in circumspect.

He is the teacher.
I take a journal of life (his and ours).

If I wrote throughout my life, once lived,
there would be a sequence; twice lived, if
read.
Mr. did not know who might drop by,
or certainly even what.
Simply accepting of all that came to him;
what comes to us.
Mr. wrote about it
and wrote again.
And I add it to my collection.

Take That, Camus — Artifact 3

Stepping from the rocks
down to the hot sand.
The glare is neither terrific nor muted,
but I am blinded the same.
Yet I can see.
Crimson stains white sand.
I find myself separate;
separating.

Two men prone (strange that the stain moves
from one?)
But their life status is of no import (but one)
They were brought upon these sands
by incident;

I am here with purpose.
It stands out even in glare
Silver and white.

Take That, Me ...? — Artifact 4

Smash it! Tear it apart!
I have destroyed an artifact and yet it lives on:
My hands are stained with the scent of myrrh.

Through my own brash actions, my attempt
to raze, I will carry the brand of which I
despise.
This scent that marks my coming.
Alabaster shards lie at my feet
marked almost separately.
Not a sound was heard.
Shaking my head I turn to go.
There will be others to take its place.

Take That, Stoppard — Artifact 5

To the man that is part beguiled,
while walking away, laughing
from two unconscious (yet well dressed)
forms
who lay prone (yet with holes in their soles)
I say to no one, "You should have examined
them before you tossed them."
Carrying both bags
I make my exeunt,
and I toss one for myself.
Still heads.

Take That, Peretz — Artifact 6

This is the moment:
Questions are raised, then answered.
I move, oblivious to them, from my hidden spot
within the close brush.
Reaching down I retrieve my prize:
a simple stool which the man from the country,
in his blind drive to seek admittance,
will believe he still occupies.

Undoubtedly, I take the only tangible thing
left of value to him.
So close to his door, I manage a glance, down
the continuing hall.
I chance to stay a moment longer, enraptured
by the possibilities of further action; curious
about the consequences of entering a door
not meant for me.

Take That, Dostoevsky — Artifact 7

From within this stand of trees, I can easily view
the Cossack
as he drives his horse, charging the retreating man.
The man stops suddenly and, hiding his burden
in the bushes, quickly marks the spot.
The Cossack reigns in before the man,
unaware of any guile,
and proceeds to berate the man for having
forgotten to sew on a hook.
They ride off together and after a moment
I deem it safe to emerge.
Reaching into the bushes,
my hand makes out the shape and texture.
I find that I am still able to smell
the aroma of the recently baked bread.

Take That, Burroughs — Artifact 8

Moving behind the men,
I am lost from their sight in the crowd.
I follow them as the source for my next
artifact:
though I have not decided yet what it will be.
I cannot make out what they say, but
suddenly all conversation between them
stops.
A naked man screams in agony, tearing at his
body as centipedes make their way out, from
within.
I am unprepared for the sight.
I had forgotten about this part, or suppressed
it.
I almost faint as a centipede, a big one,
bursts through the head of his penis.
It is a *Scolopendra* of the Andaman Islands
species which can reach 33 centimeters in
length.
This one is only 16 centimeters, but it is
enough.
As the men pass from my sight,
I grab a clay jar from the rubble.
I trap the centipede inside.
It is an ill-gotten artifact, but it will suffice.

Take That, Flaubert — Artifact 9

I wait until the churchwardens, the choristers,
and the children of the little village have gone
home.
They had come to observe a passing of sorts.
On the altar is my next prize: it is hidden
under the roses.
One of its wings is broken and the stuffing is
falling out of the stomach.
But its garish feathers still feel as if it were
still alive.
Fellacher had done a fine job.
I look up at the house.
Blue smoke still hangs in the cool night air.

Take That, Beckett — Artifact 10

I've gone too far with this game of mine
which I use to amuse my wardening.
My artifacts are never missed, but
this time I have changed the outcome.
And that is not my place.

The man rests in my chair, confused.
I offer him tea.
He speaks no words, as his eyes dart about at
what must be marvels to him.
As I recall it was with me when I
assumed this post.

I know what must be done, but
hesitate.
I offer tea again.
I lay a blanket across his lap.
Pat his shoulder reassuringly.
And offer tea again.
Which he takes and
motions for an extra lump.
I shake my head in reply.
There is already enough sugar
laced
within.

2012. Right.

Mind melting under the heavy weight of
watermelon.
Which brings us to see which witch is what,
why morsels of beef bargain attic sales
contemplate the life long indenture of typing.
We are the world, all aboard the chicken gravy
only please and if you wish to smoke please
wait until the captain has turned off the no
suicide sign.
For sooth, 'tis an evil cat shoe upon my plate.
'Tis an undertow of Traebaeshmet.
I wait upon the edge of my reality
only to contemplate the existence of
green jello
swimming in an offal of giddiness.
Someone get that, will you?
Understanding reasons for tsunamis amongst
giants.
The moon changes from quarter to half pound
and conscious design begins to
reevaluate the process of making meatloaf.

Running running running
toward neverending vwallybonger
running
for president of a very prestigious
nightmare company
of which Caspar Weinberger is a shareholder.
How's about you and me continue
this on top of magic mountains of
mouthing sludge breath
for score and seven parcel post
lined in huge
hula hoop for sale.
Want someone to take a hop
at the corner stop shop
lifting up a heavy weight
is a common factor of
zero is a placeholder
for pots and pans of Denmark.
The London Syphilis Harmonica Orchestra
opens its door is a jar of peanut butter jam
ming dynasty into a door that won't give half
penny loafer

sans moo-lah-tee doh
which will bring us back home
home on the range top stove
warming honey bakers onion roll
ing down a drain,
piping along the furrow.

*Spend enough time on the patio of a cafe, in a
busy city, next to a bus stop, and you pick up
some weird shit.*

Abide My Love

Abide my love; Abide, so long abide.
Stay lain my love, wherein the place you died.

Tonight I dig for you this grave so deep;
This grave I fill with love, and dirt, and you.
With grief I pack the dirt so you will keep;
You should have said those two small words: I d

You'd not lived up to my expectations.
But O! you certainly did in dying—
With your screams I felt exhilarations!
To say not would certainly be lying.

So now I give to you my hearts fare well;
That heart's fair well that split you at the seams.
Now I go to find myself a new belle,
One that I hope will live up to my dreams.

One semester in college, I was in a Horror Lit class and a class on Shakespeare. We had to write a sonnet for the Shakespeare one and the Horror Lit class found its way in. So... an upside-down and dark sonnet it is!

I have a word

I have a word that is solely my own.
Other people use it, and often too,
but I don't mind all that much.
To be clear though,
it belongs to me in a very real and legally-
binding sense.
I say it, write it, and show it off.
Perhaps I should introduce myself with it to
all whom I meet.
It is a word that can be used in dactylic
hexameter, or iambic pentameter, or as
change in an expired parking meter.
When I am burned at the stake my ashes will
form this word.
Every single person in the world can guess.
Look in the dictionary—or hold a seance—to
find out what it is.
And eventually they will find it.
But I'll not tell where.
To the ones who know it—and cherish it,
too—I smile and nod slightly with approval.
To the rest, I shall be kind and offer a hint:
It is not written here.

Social Media

You do not get a pass, ass
Holier than thou
Ought to put in your head
Ache that others feel
Elect to ignore
A most obvious truth
Full of self-hate
Red state, blue state
Mention again your selfish
Necessity to irrational
Eyes unopened

They're All Linden Trees

elle mettre tranquillité
à côté de moi dessous
l'arbre tilleul

les collines roulis entretenues vers nous, déferler
vert
herbeux barre à notre pied
et le soleil d'après-midi mettre chaleureux à
notre visages

she lays beside me
quietly beneath
the linden tree

the hills roll steadily toward us crashing green
grass surf at our feet
and the late afternoon sun warms our faces

We went on a touristy, but fun, bicycle tour of Versailles. Our tour guide, an Irish fellow, told us a story about the trees surrounding the palace. On a previous tour, a very young child asked what kind of tree was next to him. "It's a linden tree." And that kind? "Also a linden tree." And that one? "Linden." What about this one? "They're all linden trees!" I dunno. It made me laugh.

Ode to Whatshername

I looked at her and how closely she stood to
him,
how she said "Hi" in that particular way, and
how she leaned in to him when he spoke.

I realized how much it bothered me
when I found I was drinking
coffee gone cold
and not flinching.

Raven Brought the Sun

Before time was wise
Before earth knew rain
Before trees grew tall
Before animals knew grain
The sun did not shine in the skies.

No sparkles on the water
No rays to warm the clay
No light to coax the flowers
No morning to make bright the day
There was no Sun to balance Moon's motion.

Raven knew that Moon was lonely
She took to flight and climbed so high
On rainbow wings to guide her way
Her melodic voice that made Moon sigh
Moon gave safe perch to Raven only.

Raven sang to Moon, "Why are you sad?
Please tell me why your face does wain."
"I miss my brother Sun," cried Moon,

"And feel I search for him in vain.
To see him in my skies again would make me
so glad."

"Then I shall search everywhere for him.
From the depths of earth to the heights of
space.
I shall not rest until he is found.
I will take up the quickest pace
Through dust of earth and dust of stars I'll
swim."

Raven sprang from Moon to rainbow-winged
flight
Up and out to the constant dark.
Raven searched and searched
In hopes of finding Sun's constant spark
She sang out sweetly for him to balance the
night.

Raven was long on wing and far from earth
When at last her song reached Sun's ear.

But as she flew to Sun's hidden place,
Her bright, beautiful feathers did sear
She could find no place on Sun, like Moon, to
berth.

Raven tried to sing Moon's message out to
Sun
But Sun's heat caused her voice to crack
Her song was gone and she could but croak
"Sister Moon wants brother Sun back."
Bright feathers she'd lost, but day's light she'd
won.

Raven took Sun to turn earth's sky blue
But paid a price to bring Moon a brother
Her role in this world has been here set true.
With coal-black wings and voice like no other.

M'beo

M'beo the rain god rises
(chair)
above we three.

We prance and chant
our fearful ways about the
(colored paper)
fire
we hope
and fear
will be drenched by
(spray bottle)
rain.

O, how we praise and raise up this god,
his eyes
(sunglasses)
darkened.
Seeing, yet unseen.

Totem
(butcher paper and ink)
on his chest.

How will we be graded
(Rain or A's)?

Our
(class presentation)
ceremony
could bring both.

We have created a myth as a step towards
(standard high school diploma)
freedom.

An Ode to Sophie or It Was Short Notice and All I Had Was This Egg of Glow-in-the-Dark Silly Putty Which I Found at the Back of the Junk Drawer. Plus This Poem. Apparently.

You said, "Hey, world, it's my birthday!"
So I got you this gift.
Except your birthday was actually last
Monday.
About my timing, you're quite rightly miffed.

But this present's the answer,
I guarantee it will please.
Of course it might give you cancer.
Or a bad cough and mild wheeze.

Barring medical complications
I wish to now say:
(with flourish and felicitations)
"Happy Late Birthday!"

Sometimes, you end up getting someone a last-minute present. From the junk drawer.

First Words

My first word
(if you believe anything my parents say on the
subject of, "When Matthew was a kid...")
was Dayee.
Apparently, I pointed at the Siamese cat that
was lying in the dryer
on the warm laundry
and shouted, "Dayee, Dayee!"
Not Mommy or Daddy.
Dayee.

Daisy, to pronounce it correctly (I've come so
far),
was one of nine or ten cats that lived with my
parents and then with me when I came along.
She lived the longest.
I don't remember the others.
I only remember Daisy and
I only remember her in the dryer.

My first words
when I got the job were,
"Thanks for this opportunity. I really
appreciate this."
I really emphasized "really."
But I thought,
"Do I really want to make a living doing this?
With him?"
Once again emphasizing "really."
I was shaking his hand
and smiling.
He was smiling too.
I thought, "Do I really want this job?"
I had struggled,
as in jumping through many hoops,
to get to this point.
This handshake.
This damn smiling.

When he first reached out,
it took him 4 weeks to get back to me.
When I interviewed he said,

"You sound perfect for the job. I'll call you
tomorrow."
Of course, he never called.
I went back.
"Slipped my mind, I'll call tomorrow!"
And of course, he never called.
I called again.
"He's not here."
I called again.
"I'll give him the message."
I called again.
"To leave a message, press one..."
I gave up.
At the time I said,
"Who needs it? It's a pisser job anyway,
right?"
Everyone agreed with me, as friends do.

And then he called.

"Never got the messages. Lost your app.
Finally found it when I opened a different

folder and there you were. Can we set a time
to talk about scheduling?"

I said yes, and went over right away.
Finally, a job—after ten months with no
work.
A schedule I liked.
Good benefits.
Pleasant atmosphere.
And there I was,
shaking his hand
and smiling.
And he was smiling back at me.

And then I thought
(actually took the time to think while
standing there shaking hands and smiling),
"Do I really want to make a living doing this?
With him?"

The handshake was dragging on and
the smiling was beginning to hurt.

I felt his hand start to pull away,
so I grasped tightly and smiled real big.

"I'll tell my story walkin'."
And I did.
Walk that is.
Right through the double doors.

Sometimes
(and I say sometimes because it should never
be a habit)
it's a good thing to look in the face of
genuine opportunity
and say, "Fuck no."

*Sometimes, regardless of the work environment
or the getting paid, you know when you will be
taking on a bad boss. I've had the experience
often enough now that, if possible, given my
other responsibilities, I know I should run. There
are very few situations where it will ever be
worth it.*

My first words
when she told me she was pregnant were not
exactly what she wanted to hear.

"Finally, now I can sail off to some other place
to continue my dream of having a family in
every port."

She did laugh, but was quick to point out that
wasn't my dream, and my experience with
water vessels was limited to having once
fallen out of a canoe.
She never lets me have any fun.

My first words
when I held her never happened.
I didn't speak at all.
I held her and felt...proud?
Certainly relieved.
I do not recommend emergency c-sections.
I carried her from the operating room
to the NICU.
They let me do that.
As if I would allow otherwise.
Walking there, holding
this barely breathing being,
I knew.
I knew.
I knew I would kill anyone who got in our
way.
Welcome to being a parent.

For Claire?

O Claire, O Claire I wonder where
it's you I've seen before.
Was it, perhaps, May thirteenth, there,
when I kissed you, relaxing on the floor?
No, it was another who knocked upon my
door.

Could it be, as I have guessed,
that smile you wear so well?
Which sends my memory on a magic quest
to when we danced beyond the midnight bell.
Again, no it was another who set my heart
a-threll.

But then, I guess, I'm drawn to think,
of your eyes that squint so with gray.
Those eyes draw me toward a sweetly drink
for a roll and a tumble in the hay.
Still, no it was another that led me astray.

I'm positive that I have played with your hair,

as we lay lazily in bed and cuddled.
Twisting and caressing as I lay unaware,
of a summer's end that soon became
muddled.
No, that was not you who made my heart so
befuddled.

I realize now, with some hesitation,
that I've never known you before.
I'm glad I can say, without reservation,
that I don't have to hate you anymore.
It was not you who slammed my face in the
door.

Myria

A miniature shower
wet hands
hair well groomed
I leave and see
long,
brown
hair
swishing back and forth
with the cadence of the strut
A leather jacket
black not brown
I know a pirate that
be jealous of the boots on
those long legs
Her head turns to look
A brief smile from her red lips
I follow
I sit with her
She looks back to me
and ponders
Her smile is my reward

Purposefully Bad Haiku

Percolator drips
I drink the acidic juice
the sun warms my face

The curve of her neck
curiosity, unclothed
like wanton velvet.

Street junk clogs my veins
the whirr of Armeggedon
my guns protect me.

Blindly, light finds me.
Amorphous, fragile numbing
Tentative struggle.

Bananas hanging
China's Andy Worhol is
here eating some pie.

She is still with me.
It's been more than fifty years,
midnight farts and all.

*When you've been out drinking too much and
you challenge everyone at the table to write the
worst haiku.*

Take This Poem (with a dash of salt)

O, spiteful clam
that spat upon me;
into the pot you go.

Boiling,
twisting,
swimming
death—
there is no sand
in which to burrow.

O, cooking clam
that rolls before me,
the water amplifies your cries.
But you pissed me off
when you tired to spit
clam juice into my eyes.

I turn deaf ear
and smiling mouth
to chop

potato and carrot.
add
corn and
perhaps peas.

With a teaspoon of this,
a dash of that,
and a pinch of pepper
which makes me sneeze.

But now, conundrum:
Shall it be milk? No!
Better yet, cream.

For illustrious, if infuriating,
shellstock
such as you
less than the best I would not dream!

Wert thou an oyster,
I would simply shuck thee
and sup.
(Wert thou a mussel,

would I massage thee?)
Wert thou a scallop,
I would sauteé thee quickly
in garlic and butter.
For no other shellfish
would I go to such extreme.

Truly, I glorify the clam
I worship it supreme.
Why else go to such trouble?

"Mix other ingredients in a large pan,
withholding the cream. Clams continue
at a rolling bubble."

Mixing and boiling,
adjusting the flame,
I can smell that success is near.
The base is soon done,
"Now add the cream."

At the aroma, I shed a slight tear.
I pour in the cream and tell you that
"Other clam's would die for this cause!"
The irony hits me
like an iron.
But I give myself a polite round of applause.

Give it one last stir
then slap on the cover.
I hover with wide open eyes.
"Simmer for twenty,"
then dish up a-plenty.
Clam Chowder, my boy, is your prize!

Letter-to-the-Editor, December 1997

I walked in on the conversation,
or was it a speech?
She was saying,
"…and if that's the armpit, then Anchorage is
the butthole. It sucks up here."
Blah, blah, blah…

But, I played along.
I should have told her to leave
if she hated it so much.

So far this winter I have scraped
the outside of the windshield about 10 times.
I've scraped the inside of it almost everyday.

We went for a drive and it was
colder in the car than outside.
We went skiing and it rained.

Some people seem to think that
by owning a 4x4

they can drive four times faster than in a
regular car.
Of course, I would too.

We slip on the walkway,
scrape windows, and
drive cars that warm up only
when we get to where we're going.

We layer up clothing and waddle around.
We ask questions like, "You mean suicide is
an answer?"
We endure the darkness,
the cold,
the strange weather,
the angry retail workers, and
ask more questions like,
"Why didn't I train this dog to shit in the
toilet?!"

And we endure it all for what?

We endure it for the small mounds of snow
that cover the last piles of leaves.
For every snowball thrown,
up to the one that connects with our heads.
For snow angels and speeding innertubes.
For the squealing child and
hesitant dog experiencing their first snowfall.

We do it for the no-sound of falling snow.

So walk your dog, and
shovel the driveway.
Scrape, shiver, and slip.
And leave if you don't understand what it is
all about.

Im Possible

I never want to hear impossible
from you
I only want to hear it's possible
from you
There's always something we can do
to set things right
There's always something left to try
when the end's in sight
Giving up now is giving up too soon
Even though it feels like you have control
If you have until midnight why give up at
noon
Every moment between is what you control
I never want to hear impossible
from you
I only want to hear it's possible
from you

Final Poem

I am an artist, yet I have never
put brush to canvas.
I am a musician, yet I have never
played a single note.
I am a writer, yet I have never
written a word.

Unfortunately

"The sky is blue as far as I can see. The trees are green and yellow and red and brown. The grass is brown and green, but not growing in most parts."

I tell him it's fall.

The last time he spoke, he said hello and told me that he was four. I said that I knew that already, and he said, "Me, too." His name is K. and he is now four and a half.

K. has been resting in this bed, in this place, for over a year now. I say resting because his mother gets angry whenever I say coma.

In all the time K. has been here, he has woken from resting only twice. The first time I was here, and the short conversation that I mentioned was all that took place before he went back to sleep. The second time came when I was away on a business trip. I heard about it from the nurse that was on duty at the time.

"He must have actually gotten up," she explained, "because his feeding tubes had been taken out and he was wearing one of his slippers. When I went to check on him, he had already lapsed back into the coma."

A brief smile crossed my face as I recalled the One Slipper philosophy. Whenever I would go to tuck him in at night, I'd have to remind him to brush his teeth. He would put on one of his slippers, ones that sported a polar bear face on the toes, and hop on his one foot to the bathroom.

When I asked him why such an elaborate production, he replied, "It takes less time to put on one slipper, and if I hop all the way I get exercised, see?"

"Of course," I replied, knowing it is next to impossible to argue with kid logic.

Now I sit and watch and wait.

Wait for K. to wake up and tell me about his

dream; but he doesn't move. This entire room feels blank. I am its only source of color, even though the color is gray. White walls, white sheets, white instruments and machines, white slippers, and my kid is the whitest of all. There is no trace of the pink cheeks that would run through the house after playing in the sun all day.

"Come in, please," says K.'s doctor politely.

The wall behind his desk is plastered with diplomas and degrees from clinics and universities around the world. The doctor takes to his comfortable-looking chair, while K.'s mother and I sit in uncomfortable chairs opposite him.

"I'm afraid that the prognosis for your son's recovery is rather bleak. Since his second awakening in late August, he has taken a turn for the very worst."

K.'s mother interrupts, "Is our son going to die?"

This is the first time since our divorce that K.'s mother has referred to him as "our son." And now we are faced with no longer having our son.

"I'm sorry, but as of two hours ago, when we called you both in, we had stopped receiving any evidence of brain activity. I'm afraid we have exhausted all of our options."

Here it comes, I can feel it.

"I wanted to explain to you what your options are at this point. And there are, as I can see it, only two: he can stay on the machines, almost indefinitely, or..."

I ask, "Is there any chance that he will recover?"

The doctor purses his lips. He seems perturbed at another interruption.

"Your other option is to release him from the care of this facility."

There is nothing more we do for him. We will always be his parents, but now we must give him peace and let him fully die. I cannot say who is less fortunate, my son for having to miss all that a full life has to offer, or me and his mother who have to live the rest of our lives without him.

Unfortunately, only time will tell.

I haven't shared this with many people since I captured it in September 1992. 30 years later, I think it's okay.

(the end)

Poetry Works, Mostly

poems good enough
for the likes of you

because you're
awesome

by matthew oliphant

Acknowledgment

These poems were created while residing on the lands of the people of the Dena'ina Ełnena, Coast Salish, Multnomah, and the Ikirakutsum Band of the Shasta Nation. It is clear that genocide made this book possible and while I wish that were not the case—and I know that I am not directly responsible—I do benefit from centuries of terror, abuse, and lies by people who look exactly like me. I don't know how to address such an inhumane outcome, but addressing it must begin with acknowledgment.

About the Author

I wanted to be a poet. Then I got a job that paid me money. Stoopid capitalism. It took a couple decades to figure out I could do both. And here we are.

Boring Bio Bit

When not talking about himself in third-person, Matthew is happy to be returning to writing after a 20 year break. He currently lives with his family in Portland, Oregon and is working on another book just for you. Who knows where he is now or of what he is yet to dream.

Please buy my first book, What Did You Get Me? at *matthewoliphant.com/WDYGM*

And the next one which is out soon.

One Last Thing

Do me a favor.
Take good care of yourself.
Right now.
Seriously.

www.ingramcontent.com/pod-product-compliance
Lightning Source LLC
LaVergne TN
LVHW052031080426
835513LV00018B/2270